CW00538630

THE LITTLE
BOOK OF
SHIT

THE LITTLE BOOK OF SHIT

This edition copyright © Summersdale Publishers, 2024
First published as *The Meaning of Shit*, 2013
Also published as *The Little Book of Shit*, 2018

Poo icon © Lisa Yen/Shutterstock.com

An Hachette UK Company
www.hachette.co.uk

Summersdale Publishers Ltd
Part of Octopus Publishing Group Limited
Carmelite House
50 Victoria Embankment
LONDON
EC4Y 0DZ
UK

www.summersdale.com

Printed and bound in China

ISBN: 978-1-83799-231-7

Substantial discounts on bulk quantities of Summersdale books are available to corporations, professional associations and other organizations. For details contact general enquiries: telephone: +44 (0) 1243 771107 or email: enquiries@summersdale.com.

THE LITTLE
BOOK OF
SHIT

summersdale

CONTENTS

· · · · · · · · · · · · · · · · · · ·

PHILOSOPHICAL
SHIT

EXISTENTIALISM

· ·

Shit happening
is absurd.

FATALISM

. . . .

Shit is going
to happen.

FEMINISM

• •

We want the same
shit as men.

FETISHISM

. . . .

I love it when
shit happens.

HEDONISM

· ·

There's nothing quite
like a good shit.

MASOCHISM

Shit on me.

NIHILISM

· ·

This shit
has no meaning.

OPTIMISM

· ·

This shit is pretty good.

PESSIMISM

· ·

Shit sucks.

POLITICAL
CORRECTNESS

· ·

Heavily processed
nutritionally deprived
biological output happens.

PROCRASTINATION

• •

I'll shit tomorrow.

SADISM

· ·

I will shit on you.

STOICISM

· ·

This shit doesn't
hurt at all.

VEGETARIANISM

· ·

If it shits,
don't eat it.

THALES

Earth, Air, Fire
and Shit.

SOCRATES

· ·

What is shit?
Why is shit?

EPICURUS

· ·

If shit happens,
enjoy it.

ARCHIMEDES

Hmm... why doesn't
this shit float?

RENÉ DESCARTES

• •

I shit, therefore I am.

FRIEDRICH NIETZSCHE

· ·

Shit is dead.

SIGMUND FREUD

Shit is a phallic symbol.

ERWIN SCHRÖDINGER

· ·

This simultaneously is
and is not shit.

JEAN-PAUL SARTRE

· ·

Shit is other people.

KURT GÖDEL

• • • • • • • • • • • • • • • • • • • •

It can be proved that
it cannot be proved
that shit happens.

SCIENTIFIC SHIT

ASTRONOMER

• •

Look at all that
shit in the sky.

BIOLOGIST

• •

Is this shit alive?

CHEMIST

· ·

I hope this shit
doesn't blow up.

DOCTOR

. . . .

Take two shits and
call me in the morning.

ENGINEER

. . . .

I hope this shit
holds together.

MATHEMATICIAN

· ·

You can't divide
shit by zero.

PHYSICIST (THEORETICAL)

· ·

Shit SHOULD happen.

PHYSICIST (EXPERIMENTAL)

· ·

To within experimental error,
shit DID happen.

PSYCHOLOGIST

· · · · · · · · · · · · · · · · · · · ·

And how did that shit
make you feel?

SURGEON

• •

Shit, where's this organ
supposed to go?

CHARLES DARWIN

. . . .

Survival of the shittest.

ALBERT EINSTEIN

• •

Shit is relative.

WERNER HEISENBERG

· ·

Shit happened, we just
don't know where
or how much.

NEIL ARMSTRONG

• •

One small shit for man...
One giant heap for mankind.

RELIGIOUS
SHIT

TAOISM

. . . .

Shit happens.

CONFUCIANISM

. . . .

Confucius said,
"Shit happens."

BUDDHISM

• •

If shit happens,
it isn't really shit.

ZEN

. . . .

What is the sound
of shit happening?

HINDUISM

. . . .

This shit has
happened before.

HARE KRISHNA

• •

Shit happens, shit happens, happens, happens, shit, shit...

SIKHISM

• •

This shit was revealed
by the Guru.

CATHOLICISM

. . . .

If shit happens,
you deserved it.

PROTESTANTISM

• •

If shit happens,
praise the Lord for it!

FUNDAMENTALISM

• •

If shit happens, you will
go to hell, unless you
are born again.

JEHOVAH'S WITNESSES

· ·

Good morning,
I have some shit
for you to read.

AMISH

• •

This modern shit
is immoral.

JUDAISM

• •

So shit happens,
already!

ISLAM

• •

There is no
shit but shit.

NEW AGE

. . . .

If shit happens,
honour it and share it.

VOODOO

• •

Let's stick pins
in this shit!

SATANISM

. . . .

SNEPPAH TIHS.

JEDI

· ·

May the shit
be with you.

AGNOSTICISM

. . . .

How can we KNOW
if shit happens?

ATHEISM

• •

I don't believe
this shit!

POLITICAL
SHIT

POLITICIAN

· ·

If you elect me,
shit will never
happen again.

COMMUNISM

· ·

Share the shit equally.

CAPITALISM

· ·

That's MY shit.

JULIUS CAESAR

· ·

I came, I saw, I shitted.
(*Veni, Vidi, Shitti.*)

GEORGE
WASHINGTON

· ·

I cannot tell a lie –
shit happened.

ABRAHAM LINCOLN

· ·

Four score and
seven shits ago...

FRANKLIN D. ROOSEVELT

. . . .

The only thing we
have to fear is
shit itself.

JOHN F. KENNEDY

• •

Ask not what your shit can
do for you — ask what you
can do for your shit.

BILL CLINTON

I didn't inhale that shit.

BARACK OBAMA

· ·

We are the shit
that we seek.

HENRY VIII

Off with their shit!

WINSTON
CHURCHILL

· ·

We shall shit on
the beaches.

MARGARET
THATCHER

· ·

The shit is not
for turning.

THERESA
MAY

. . . .

No shit is better
than a bad shit.

BREXIT

· ·

We send the EU
£350 million a week.
Let's fund our shit instead.

SOCIAL
SHIT

MILLENNIAL

· ·

Avocados are the shit.

GEN Z

· ·

This shit hits different.

FACEBOOK

· ·

You want to share your shit?
So do we.

TWITTER

. . . .

Your shit's got
10,000 retweets!

INSTAGRAM

· ·

Put a filter
on that shit.

TIKTOK

•••••••••••••••••••••••••

... makes me buy shit.

SNAPCHAT

• •

You have 3 seconds
to view my shit.

HIPSTER

. . . .

I liked this shit before
it was cool.

POSER

• •

I have the latest shit.

STUDENT

I'll just sleep
through this shit.

....

WORK
SHIT

....

GOOD DAYS

• •

I do this shit
for a living!

BAD DAYS

· ·

I don't get paid enough
for this shit.

APPRAISAL TIME

· ·

You're shit.

PAY
NEGOTIATIONS

· · · · · · · · · · · · · · · · · · · ·

You want
HOW MUCH shit!?

ACCOUNTS

· ·

Your shit's in the post.

ADMINISTRATION

• •

I'm sorry, but we can't make
this shit happen until you fill
out form XP1 in triplicate.

BLUE-SKY THINKING

• • • • • • • • • • • • • • • • • • • •

I like to shit
outside the box.

HEALTH
AND SAFETY

· ·

Please keep
your shit tidy.

HR

· ·

We're looking for continuous
improvement of our shit.

IT HELPDESK

Have you tried
restarting your shit?

MANAGEMENT

· ·

Shit harder!

MARKETING

•••••••••••••••••••••••••

This shit could sell,
if only it came in
different colours.

PAYROLL

· ·

You can have your shit
once a month.

CHEF

· ·

... and some shit on
the top to garnish.

DRIVING INSTRUCTOR

. . . .

When I give the signal,
I would like you to do
an emergency shit.

ECONOMIST

. . . .

I hope no one realizes
that I don't really
understand this shit.

HAIRDRESSER

· ·

Whoever cut this
last time was shit.

HISTORIAN

· ·

Shit repeats itself.

LAWYER

· ·

For a sufficient fee,
I can get you out of ANY shit.

MECHANIC

· ·

This shit's going
to cost you...

POLICE OFFICER

· · · · · · · · · · · · · · · · · · · ·

Anything you shit may be given
as evidence in court.

TEACHER

● ●

Repeat after me:
1 shit + 1 shit = ...

UNION LEADER

Give us more shit
or we'll strike.

WAITER

• •

You want fries
with that shit?

CULTURAL
SHIT

BLUES MUSIC

. . . .

Woke up this morning,
took a shit.

MINIMALISM

· ·

Shit.

PAINTING

. . . .

This is an
abstract shit.

POETRY

. . . .

The cat shat
on the mat.

ROCK MUSIC

• • • • • • • • • • • • • • • • • • • •

This shit needs a solo.

SURREALISM

· ·

Fish.

LEONARDO DA VINCI

· ·

Can you tell what
this shit is thinking?

WILLIAM SHAKESPEARE

· ·

To shit or not to shit,
that is the question.

JACKSON
POLLOCK

• •

This is what I call
action shitting.

CLARK GABLE

Frankly, my dear,
I don't give a shit.

GRETA GARBO

• •

I want to shit alone.

FRANK SINATRA

· ·

I shat it my way.

CLINT
EASTWOOD

· ·

Do you feel shit, punk?

CAPTAIN
JAMES T. KIRK

• • • • • • • • • • • • • • • • • • • •

... to boldly shit where no one
has shat before!

MR SPOCK

· ·

Shit long and prosper.

ELVIS PRESLEY

· ·

Don't shit on my
blue suede shoes.

AL PACINO

· ·

Say hello to
my little shit.

OTIS REDDING

• •

Shitting on the
dock of the bay.

ARNOLD
SCHWARZENEGGER

• • • • • • • • • • • • • • • • • • • •

Shit'll be back.

NOEL
EDMONDS

· ·

Shit or no shit?

LIONEL RICHIE

. . . .

Shitting on the ceiling.

MR T

· ·

I pity the shit.

JAMES CAMERON

• •

This shit's expensive!

DAMIEN
HIRST

• •

You can cut a shit in half,
but it's still a shit.

MICHAEL BAY

• • • • • • • • • • • • • • • • • • • •

Let's blow some shit up.

BEYONCÉ

• •

If you liked shit then you should
have put a ring on it.

RIHANNA

. . . .

You can shit under
my umbrella.

. . . .

ANIMAL
SHIT

. . . .

BEAR

• •

Do I shit in the woods?

CAT

· ·

Dogs are shit.

DOG

• •

I love all this shit!

DUNG BEETLE

· ·

This shit tastes great.

ELEPHANT

● ● ● ● ● ● ● ● ● ● ● ● ● ● ● ● ● ● ●

An elephant never
forgets to shit.

FISH

· ·

All I do is eat,
swim and shit.

MEERKAT

• •

Even my shit is cute!

PARROT

• •

Who's a pretty shit?

SEAGULL

• •

Watch out! Here
comes my shit!

SEAHORSE

. . . .

Whose shit idea was it
to single us guys out
to have the babies?

SLOTH

· ·

I would shit but
I can't be bothered.

TORTOISE

· ·

Slow and steady
wins the shit.

Have you enjoyed this book? If so, find us
on Facebook at Summersdale Publishers, on
Twitter at @Summersdale and on Instagram
and TikTok at @summersdalebooks and get
in touch. We'd love to hear from you!

www.summersdale.com